INTERSECT

Some of the poems in this book have appeared in *The Canadian Forum, Fiddlehead,* the *Antigonish Review* and *Salt.*

INTERSECT

Poems

Carol Shields

Borealis Press
Ottawa, Canada
1974

*The author wishes to thank the Canada Council
for its generous assistance.*

This book had been published with the help of a grant from the
Ontario Arts Council.

ISBN 0-919594-27-1

Cover design by Bull's Eye Design
Ottawa, Canada

Printed and bound in Canada

TABLE OF CONTENTS

Pioneers: Southeast Ontario 9
Mother 10
Friend: after Surgery 11
Aunt Alice Recalled 12
Reading In Bed 13
Woman at a Party 14
Professor 15
Suppertime 1950 16
Margaret, Aged Four 17
Service Call 18
Emily Dickinson 19
Rough Riders 20
Accidents 21
Volkswagon 22
Sister 23
After the Party: I 24
After the Party: II 25
Radio Announcer 26
Child Learning to Talk 27
A Couple Take a Sunday Drive 28
Letter From a Friend 30
William 31
Betty 32
Fetus 33
Our Mother's Friends 34
Class in Evolution 35

Couple 36
Singer 37
Homemovies 1962 38
Old Friend — Long Distance 39
Uncle 40
Helen Lighting a Fire 41
Old Men 42
Friend of a Friend 43
Picnic at the Lake 44
Daughter 45
A Couple Celebrate Their Silver Anniversary 46
Someone We Saw 47
Family Friend, Aged Ninety 48
An Actor in the Little Theatre 49
Family at the Cottage 50
Poet 51
Sunbathers: Canada 52
January 53
Boys Playing Chess 54
Neighbour 55
Carolers: Ottawa 56
Boy Waking Up 57
Circles 58
As For Us 59

Pioneers: Southeast Ontario

They existed.   Butter bowls
and hayrakes testify,
and ruined cabins
their grievous roofs
caved in.

But they're melting to myth,
every year harder to believe
in, and the further we travel away
the more we require
in the form of proofs.

Of course
you still meet those who
are old enough to
claim kinship, but eye
witnesses are scarce
now and unreliable.

We want sealers, cuttlery, clods
of earth, flames from their fires,
footsteps, echoes, the breath
they breathed,
a sign, something to
keep faith by
before they go the way
of the older gods.

Mother

While we slept our mother
moved furniture.

Through dull unfocused
dreams we could hear
the coarse scrape
of chairs and the sharp sound
of her breath easing
the sofa in place, its plush girth
opening fresh wounds
in the wallpaper.

In the morning we found
the amazing corners, startled by pure
circuits of light we'd never
seen before, pleasing
elbows of space and new shapes
to fit into   bringing us
closer to rebirth
than we ever
came   in all those years.

Friend: after Surgery

Flowers bloom
their kindest, and nurses sprout
minor rhetoric,
but rhythm is the only way out
of this dark room.

His eyes avoid the inked blurt
on the offical chart.
He's busy enough with
the diesal hum of his breath,
the electric
thunder of his heart.

Aunt Alice Recalled

Grass gags the sidewalk
    between the church
    and her place

trumpet vines
    pierce the chalk-
    white porch
    the screen door traced
    with rust

Inside   the fern-
    crushed air,
    the fainting plush of chairs
    breathing the mid-day dinner

As always she waits
    in the walls,
    filling her total space
    touching at every turn

so that nothing must
    be explained or defined

    It's all
    here

Reading In Bed

At night
lying close together
propped up by accustomed pillows
they read in a shaded slant
of yellow light.

He is intent
on his book while she browses
happily enough through magazines.

The hour narrows
that which they scarcely miss
between
them   and turning pages   their elbows
sometimes touch by accident.

They're locked into print,
paper adheres to the skin
of their sleep, and ink thins
their dreams to water
but what does it matter.

Peace like this
is an accomplishment.

Woman at a Party

A circle bursts in another
room,   a woman's voice
flutes the air with laughter.

Her pleated alto notes
pass through walls,
pierce the furniture

and like flowers fall
on our darkly-suited
selves, gathered to discuss
Belfast.
       Then
           ice cubes rejoice
in our glasses, gin buzzes throats
contageous with happiness.

We are saved tonight, and after
the party ends we float
home,   the muted
edge of that rising laughter
leading us

Professor

When he lectured
　words fell out like fruit,
　each shapely syllable locked
　into the next,
　his lips stitched with certainty
　and even the roots
　of his tiny beard
　were crisped with context.

What we heard
　we respected,
　but the hole in his sock
　made us love him.

　(pale half-moon of skin
　that fractured
　his innocent symmetry
　　changing
　　everything)

Suppertime 1950

Six o'clock. This hour
encircles itself, measured
out in voices and doors,
running water and the graceless scraping
of vegetables and showers
of steps on patterned floors.

We are so easily reassured
by mere clatter
by the sweet pleasing rise
of familiar steam   shaping
what we've more or less
come to recognize
as happiness.

Margaret, Aged Four

Locked into imagery
rare as algebra and unburdened
so far by science,
she perceives life in unlikely places.

For instance
watching the rain
and the nervous race
of windshield wipers, she explains

this one
is trying to chase
that one
out of her garden.

Just as though
the distance
between life and motion
and reality
measured zero.

Service Call

His van arrived
witty as a rooster ——
he had come to repair
our troubled telephone

From the window
we watched him race
leather-haunched up
the serious pole

And there —
leaning alone
into green-wired leaves
buzzing with gossip

he phoned from an oval
of space
pure perfect numbers
we'll never know

Emily Dickinson

Minutes hide their tiny Tears

and Days weep into Aprons.

A stifled Sorrow from the Years

And Silence from the Eons.

Rough Riders

Jogging into view supersized
in wired shoulders and thighs
attached like meat, the least
of them intent on murder,

though they surprise
us by being obedient to whistles,
lining up in tidy rows
more like goodly country lads
than contract heroes.

Huddle-time and their bums rough
out lunatic lilly pads
on the comic green.

                It's here
that they play at priests
locked in holy circles
plotting death
by number
so intricate we're glad
we came after all.

Furthermore, by sitting here
we hold the seasons still.
The sun is a striped beast,
the air just sharp enough
filling the bottom of every breath
with the rasp of winter.

Accidents

Here's a list:

a scar that licks
close to the bone   compliant
part of my skin
now   seldom noticed

our cracked and broken
teacups   penitent
on shelves   earless they're taken
along on picnics

the crushed fender
injured   resists
repair but is useful
anyway as an omen

and between us surrender

Accustomed to accidents
we're no longer even
watchful

Volkswagon

At the auto show
the original Volkswagon
is on display,
spotlit, velvet-draped,
the daddy of them all,
that same crouched shape
revolving like a prehistoric skull.

Better to forget the black
era of its origin.
Think of its prim chrome lips
instead, its likeable back,
just humble enough for humans,
the friendly hips
enclosing those well meaning
wheels, so anxious to get going,
so certain they know
the way.

Sister

Curious
the way our mother's
gestures survive
in us.

When she was alive
we never noticed
but now in the dark
opening up
since her sudden
leaving, we are more aware.

A thousand miles away in
a similar kitchen
you pause
to lift a coffee cup.

And here
my smaller identical wrist
traces the same arc,
precise in mid-morning air,

linking us together,
reminding us
exactly who she was,
who we are.

After the Party: I

Calling good-by good-by
but thinking   it's easy enough
for you, opening a blind
door on the promising dark,

but for us left behind
to forage
in this insane
quiet, nothing at all remains
of this evening.

only the ringed
print of a glass, a rough
question mark
in another language
asking what for and why.

After the Party: II

Think of us, the ones who leave,
travelling from this core
of light into the bruising
cave of weather

where all at once we
are struck by, one, the shut door,
two, the sudden cold wreathed
with silence and, three, losing
with every
step what we have so carefully
put together.

Radio Announcer

His throat is a piece of sculpture
designed for ultimate resonance.
His larynx serves the pure
mid-atlantic vibration,
vowels rolling in like vitamins
cut short by the sure
german-chop of consonants

but tasteful tasteful
pitched to avoid offense,
a public masculine
without past or future.

Though it must have been half-
sized once,
a child's voice, shrill
as a whistle.
It might have been
happy, it might even
have laughed

before it vanished
forever inside the great
humming tubes of the varnished
Philco where existence
begins at the station break.

Child Learning to Talk

Almost from the start
be uttered
knotted syllables

(miniature grammars nested in his head,
phrases burgeoning,
the verbs lined up like vegetables)

and with age
found words stuck to chairs
tables doors beds
never to come apart

and never recalling or acknowledging
that brief uncluttered
and untitled space where
he once lived on air
alone before the rain of language.

A Couple Take a Sunday Drive

Driving through these old towns
We gladly surrender our youth
And dream of a daft
Old Age   which we'll spend
In a house by the river,
A house with a skin of clapboard
Gingerbread fretting its lips
Idyllic with chestnut trees.

You'll be a Main Street Loiterer
Bringing me morsels of gossip
Delicious as candy
As well as the local lord
At war with encroaching industry.

And I'll be
A Small Town Character
With a parlor
Designed for that purpose
A reader of Marcel Proust
A writer of cranky letters
A tart old dear in amber
beads, convicted of witchcraft.

And we'll live like a pair
Of old clowns,
Snug in our gothic chamber
With turrets rising about
Us like flames of imperfect truth.

Our children will be ashamed of us
But our grandchildren without a doubt
Will write us up in essays.

We'll never give way to cancer, palsy,
Deafness, arthritis, heart-disease.
The only thing that will end
It all is the killing clout
Of sanity.

Letter From a Friend

What do you mean you don't
understand me these days?
Can't you see I'm
sewn up with sadness?
Stitched through and through with grief that won't
be comforted or identified.

Damn you, you were always
one to minimize: hormones
you finally decide
as an excuse
for my bitch-madness.

Let me alone.
Something terrible inside
me has come loose.
Give me time.

William

He's fifteen now and harmless.
At night he roams the kingdom
of our back lane between
garbage cans and cars,
in love with the breath of gasoline,
his poor brain smashed in some
stone-age accident.

He sometimes runs like a featherless
hen, head thrown back, wings bent,
yelping above the screen
of permitted sound, leaping
the roof of our sleeping
house and coaxing a referendum
from the old and faithful stars.

Betty

You can hardly remember
a season ago, a century ago
when you, faithful on your knees,
placed these papery bulbs in
earth.   Dry things, colloquial
as onions, but even then
their crackling skins
rustled with knowledge.

Now with nothing of winter
left but a few
grey collars of snow
around the larger trees,
already the tulips poke through,

    showing their tutored stems, their formal
    turbaned heads, and at the edge
    of every petal
    the remembering ridge
    of origin.

Fetus

Out of absence
the snail-curved
spine has grown
another centimeter.

Darkness is more
than climate here.
It has substance
and dimension.

Its dense-walled centre
spins bone on bone
links blank tendons
to blind nerves,

and never dreams or senses
what pours
daily from the unknown
impossible eye of the sun.

Our Mother's Friends

Before
us, before our
father even,
our mother's friends
were,

their brownish photographed lives
tender in legends
floating loose between flowers
and locks of hair.

Mary Organ the county beauty
pregnant and unmarried
at twenty jumped
from the top of a player
piano to the parlor floor
where she died
poor Mary Organ

And Grace with a stump
foot and the face
of an angel, her wheelchair
a fixture
on country roads, brave Grace.

And our favourite Lily
mere fragment she survives
for one reason only
her signature
Lovingly
L – i – ly

34

Class in Evolution

We sit in a circle of chairs
books open on our laps, we are
doing Darwin this week, tracing his innocent
maps of order all the way
to the cloudless solution,

watching what had waited transparent
all those fumbling years
fall open like a garden flower,
step by step confusion
closed by theory.

And no clause left for accident.
Beneath his patterned stars
it is a matter of destiny
with doomed orders huddled together
as the earth's edge, their time done.

Now we are sent, the appointed ones,
bookeating swallowing species
hungering circular monster
lunching on reasons
for being here.

Couple

Eleven o'clock
news   sports   weather
then the final
checking of the doors

At this hour the curtains refuse
even moonlight
and the dark stairs
exhausted by ritual
complain through carpet

You reach for the clock
and choose
the hour of our waking while
I adjust the bright
degrees of our blanket

The sheets slide back
We move together

Singer

Three-quarters drunk, late at night
across the subway platform, waiting
for the last train home, he swayed
serenely between two friends.

Their elbows dared
him, urging him forward
three lurching steps where he paused,
composed his hands and, self-appointed,
began to sing,

astonishing the air
with a crimson baritone, brandy-sweet,
touching us, touching even
the station roof with sound.

At the end
a Caruso bow and a bright
crack of applause
before the train came hurtling in.

From there we travelled across
the city while music unwound
to our destinations.

       It stayed
with us, carrying us on toward
the glittering transfer points,
humming in the final buses
to the veins of our jointed streets,
small as needles in the moonlight,
and still singing.

Homemovies 1962

In those days even
the sky
we smiled in
was lighter than air

hardly able to
hold the thin
waving of our hands,
but it's all there

      you
      circled in sun
      shaping a question,
      and I
      moving my head less
      than a fraction
      of an inch   answer
         yes

Old Friend — Long Distance

By choice
we touch through wire now,
feeling our way
down the blue
looped lies
of electricity.

What we do say
we squander
since I hardly recognize
the coastline of your voice
and you don't know how
to deal with my hesitations.

       No wonder
you don't understand me
No wonder I can't hear you.

Uncle

When he speaks
it is with the privileged
angular paragraphs
of old essays,
his phrases antique
and shapely as jewellry.

But when he laughs
he touches new territory
somewhere sad between
language and breath
just missing the edge
of what he really
means.

Helen Lighting a Fire

We watch while
a match is offered and received

and a fire starts.
She burns twigs, leaves,
the sad feet
of old shrubs, the wrists
of young trees.

Fluent
she whispers to the blue-
footed twist
of flame, transparent
as lace

and sees
logs snap joyful in two,
their tough sudden hearts
enclosing the heat
and lighting her face
with a smile
or something like a smile.

Old Men

First to come
the disabling treachery
of language

the slow spaced notes
of speech that detach
themselves and words that freeze
up suddenly   so much for wisdom

then the surprised foliage
of age
hoarse phrases that catch
in folded throats

beg your pardon please
if you will please
excuse me allow me permit me
help me forgive me please please

Friend of a Friend

A stranger
listed in my address
book, friend of a friend,
his name a gift given
in a time of famine.

The address is useless
now, a street without a city,
but I keep his smudged
name. Why not? It is a hedge
against disaster and, who knows, he
may love me someday or lend
me money or rescue me
in a time of danger.

Also, it is not impossible
that he carries my name
too, friend of a friend,
his claim on me as final
as mine on him.

Picnic at the Lake

We are posed for a painting,
arranged under a formal
tempera sky,
our thermos and fruit
colourful on cloth, the grass
around us green as Astro-Turf.

Behind us
little boats salute
each other, gay as vaudeville
on a stippled surf
inside a polished frame.

You and I
freeze on the surface
where we are waiting

where we are waiting
under a skin of glass
to be explained

Daughter

We've seen
her pull spoons from empty air,
small scattered notes, absolute
as coinage,

the pewter sound
of her flute
carrying her further and further
away so that often we
lose sight of her
completely.

The rapid rising stairs
of her breath astonish
our house, and the hemorrhage
of silver, netted like fish,
falls on private ground
where we've never really
been.

A Couple Celebrate
Their Silver Anniversary

For some time now
we've been out of focus.
What was easy between us
once is cold as calculus.

Our nerve ends
scratch, selfish as hens
but all we can do
is make new bargains.

I let
   you love me.
You allow
   me to love you.
There may be
   surprises yet.

Someone We Saw

One summer evening we saw
(incredible) on a patch
of old front
lawn, a young man sitting
barechested at an ironing board.

He was typing with such
speed   his urgent
hands swatting mosquitoes
between the lines.
He never looked up, of course.

It was, well, absurd.
There must be a law
somewhere which
prohibits this kind
of thing, and what's worse,
we didn't know
a single word
of what he was writing.

Family Friend, Aged Ninety

Where did it come from
this circus crush of colour?

The room where she sits
shakes with it,
the walls breaking with staggered garlands
the carpet deranged by pattern
Even the television vibrates
with garish daytime rainbows

She would be overcome
if she didn't concentrate
instead on her plaster hands,
estranged and bare as Lent in her lap

               Bloodless
her lips blow
this dancing parlor
out of existence while her eyes turn
in to pre-selected darkness

An Actor in the Little Theatre

Last year he starred
in Death of a Salesman.
Now whitened and whiskered
he has grown heroic,
his shoulders squared
with authentic valour.
his phrases supple with intellect.

He is rehearsed
into bravery,
the colour
of his disposition
magically reversed.

The effect
is hypnotic
but our clapping hands
release to a question
    Who is he?

Family at the Cottage

The partitions are half up now,
bony structures
of two-by-fours marking
off where the rooms will be

Nothing is quite normal —
wires complicate the rafters
and the bathtub, white-sided cow
sits boastful with fittings

The children, dazed by novelty,
pass supernatural
through walls

and at night
we fall
asleep in exotic lumbered corners
almost touching but never quite

Poet

For years we
read everything he
wrote

which is why
tonight we are
diminished by
his handshake

dismembered
by the bitter
minerals of his throat

a form of treason
it will take
longer to forget than
it did to remember

Sunbathers: Canada

Sunbathers, lotus-eaters,
all day lie
oiled and glistening
in the sweet boiled eye
of the sun   listening
to fierce tenor
tunes of heat

just as though
this were the land
of paradise

but they know
better   their inner ear
is pierced by a splinter
of ice
and they can hear
through the skeptical sand
the serious heartbeat
of winter
the puritan feather-falling snow

January

OOOOOOOOooooooooo
everyone in this house is sick
everyone   all the furniture
is depressed   even the clever
armchair so recently recovered

we must we must
do something about these walls
they are so weary of it all,
the piano's unfit
and those varnished beasts gathered
in the diningroom are suicidal,
little wonder, and the carpets are chronic

only the dishwasher is really
well   the machinery
of its blue watcrfalls
cheerful as ever
its pure cycles admonish us
we hatc it

Boys Playing Chess

They'll grow old
    these young boys hunched intent
    over a chess board.

Already they have the gestures
    of old men, the hesitation of hands
    hooked in air over castles and pawns
    prefiguring their futures,

each forward thrust and turn
    pre-recorded.
    From here on
    all moves are planned,

and though they can't see or understand
    and would grieve to be told,
    there's nothing left to learn
    now but a fringe of refinement.

Neighbour

From across the street
we see her scissored
off by walls.
A hand quick as a lizard
takes in the milk
and once a week a sheet
weeps on the line.
That's all that's all
there is so why envy her?

Nutty old maid   spinster
crazy woman crazy woman
her silhouette balloons on silk
tassled blinds
private as a witch or a wizard
or a goddess, letting no one in,
choosing – that's the word   choosing no one.

Carolers: Ontario

Their songs are circular,
voices etched
visible in the breath
of this colder country,

colder than that scratched
land where nothing grows
but a mad flowering of myth,

colder by far than Europe with
its stoney saviours prayerful
in doorways.

All the more remarkable
that they sing
here,   lunatic in snow
under these freezing local stars,

feeling their way
back toward the exact
centre where history
and miracle intersect
announcing another beginning.

Boy Waking Up

He woke
before the yellow rim
of the sun

and by accident
the whole realm
of existence slid
into view for one
moment

stretched under eyelids
blinding and extravagant
as film

drowning him
in a single stroke

Circles

Driving home in the dark
in the blue bridal
path of snowplows

watching circles flow
from overhead arc
lights, the pattern cut.

The shape selects
me like the moon
and I perceive my
journeys rounded by
departures and arrivals.

The brain plots angles
corners edges but

survival
clings to the perfect
curve of seasons.

As For Us

Why can't we live like
    this old clock,
    sure of our polished skin,
    set in motion by a careful key,

all our knowledge coiled in
    one accomplished spring, its wound-
    up heart, its slow
    and calculated
    letting go,

our accurate hands pulled round and round
    every day completed
    every hour a victory.

• Cap-Saint-Ignace
• Sainte-Marie (Beauce)
Québec, Canada
1997

« L'IMPRIMEUR »